To

_____

From

_____

Date

_____

Praise for *40 Rules Every Sales Pro Needs to Know*

"Gregg Jackson is a consummate sales professional who has consistently delivered results, regardless of the territory, company or product. This book is ideal for the novice to tenured, given the competitiveness of today's selling environment combined with the necessary foundation to succeed. Sales representatives today can no longer sell on relationships alone!"

Kim Bridges Rodriguez, CEO, Acessa Health Inc.

"Gregg Jackson is truly one of the best sales professionals I've had the pleasure of working with. Watching Gregg operate with his customers—internal and external—was always impressive. Gregg has lived his book out and I hope it is a huge success!"

Scott Drake, President and CEO, Spectranetics Inc.

"I enjoyed the book. The 40 Rules covers numerous common sense suggestions, clearly articulated and supported by personal experience from one of the best. These anecdotes should serve as good reminders for any sales professional to hone their craft and help elevate them to a true 'Sales Pro.' Reading and implementing these suggestions on a consistent basis will pave the way for being the best."

Dick Cassidy, Sr. Vice President, Argon Medical Devices

"Gregg Jackson personifies the sales professional. He's a no nonsense, no excuses, right to the point sales professional who truly lives out the 40 rules in this book. This book is a great reminder for tenured sales professionals and a must read for new sales professional. Gregg is a man of faith and integrity; coupled with the 40 rules, it's no wonder he's among the best of the best."

Marc Toth, CEO, ACA Cardiovascular

"Gregg Jackson's new book provides an excellent summary of the essential characteristics exhibited by the top sales professionals in any industry. In a business world that is constantly changing and getting more complex every day, these characteristics have stood the test of time."

Thomas R. Trotter, former President and CEO of AngioScore

"Some people say sales professionals are born not made. Gregg provides valuable insight which he has honed over his long and successful career which can be learned by anyone wanting to become a sales pro. Of course, there are intangibles like hard work, honesty, integrity, character and authenticity. Gregg displays these characteristics, too! He has made a commitment to his craft and has enjoyed perennial accolades because he is a true sales pro. I have personally witnessed Gregg live out his advice and I've watched customers stay loyal because he is genuinely thinking win, win with these methods in every sale!"

Jason Bottiglieri, CEO, Infraredx

40 rules
every **SALES PRO**
needs to know

the top sales
techniques
practices &
habits of elite
SALES PROS

national best-selling author
gregg jackson

Copyright © 2018 by Gregg Jackson

ISBN: 978-1-5323-7481-4

Printed in the United States of America

www.greggjackson.com

JAJ Publishing

All rights reserved. No part of this book may be transmitted in any form or by any means, electronic or mechanical, including photocopying, recording, or by any information storage or retrieval system, in part, in any form, without the permission of the author.

Contents

	Dedication ix
	Introduction xi
1	Use The Front Door 1
2	Humility is Key 3
3	Bring Value to Every Customer... 5
4	Appropriate Follow Up is Key 7
5	Failure to Prepare is Preparation for Failure 9
6	If You Can't Say It In 4 Words of Fewer, Don't Say It 11
7	Cultivate Partnerships Not Customers................................ 13
8	Successful Leaders Serve Others 15
9	Show Gratitude... 17
10	After You Close The Deal, Shut Up..................................... 19
11	People Buy From People They Like.................................... 21
12	Focus on Your Customer's Pain Points............................... 23
13	Less Telling More Selling 25
14	Sales is a Process Not An Event 27
15	Always Have Lots of Irons in the Fire.................................. 29
16	Never Criticize Your Competition.. 31
17	Know the Decision Maker 33
18	You Don't Need to Kick the Door Down. Just Get a Foot In It 35
19	Attitude Determines Altitude... 37
20	Half-Heartedness Always Results in Defeat....................... 39
21	Always Acknowledge and be Respectful of Customer's Time... 41
22	Never Be at a Loss for Words 43

23	Always Be Prepared to Discuss, "What's New" With Your Customers	45
24	Eye Contact is Vital	47
25	People Love to Hear Their Own Name	49
26	Superficial Discussions Usually Result in Superficial Understanding	51
27	Rejection is Normal in Sales	53
28	Asking the Right Questions Provides an Opportunity to Inform and Educate	55
29	Set 1-2 Minor Goals Daily and Accomplish Them Before Noon	57
30	Simplify the Sales Process	59
31	Person to Person Communication is Generally Always the Best	61
32	Optimize "Down Time."	63
33	Minimize Power Point Whenever Possible	65
34	Focus on Common Interests and Experiences with Your Customers	67
35	Be Open and Ask for Constructive Criticism from your Customers and Colleagues	69
36	Have Difficult Conversations With Your Customers	71
37	Be Nice Even When You Don't Feel Like It	73
38	Find Out What the Most Successful Sales Reps With Whom You Work Are Doing	75
39	Be Your Own Unique Self	77
40	Don't Gossip and Associate With Negative Teammates	79

Dedication

This book is dedicated to the love of my life, my wife Annie, whose encouragement, support and love has always been a huge source of all the success I've ever enjoyed in my business and sales career.

Introduction

Millions of sales professionals work to earn a living around the globe every day.

But very few are actual Sales Pros.

A sales professional is somebody who is paid to sell a product or service.

Sales Pros are the best of the best.

Not only do they earn a living in sales, but in most cases, the best of the best Sales Pros earn a handsome living! These are the upper echelon…the top 1% of consistent over-achievers who consistently outperform the competition and win all the prestigious awards year after year.

So, are these Elite Sales Pros just blessed with an inherent know how? Did they just inherit the rare "sales gene?"

I do believe that the most Elite Sales Pros do actually possess many personality and character traits that are common among the most successful sales people.

However, based on my own 25-plus years in sales and sales management in consumer products, hi-tech and the medical device industry, I've noticed that the most successful sales people with whom I've worked, managed and been around also regularly incorporate a lot of the same techniques, practices and habits which enable them to achieve success on a consistent basis.

Success that most of their colleagues and competitors rarely achieve.

The book lists the top 40 techniques and tips that no matter what industry you work in you can incorporate and apply to make you more successful as well.

I've learned the techniques, practices and habits in this book through many successes and, yes, many failures too. Applying these vital "learned lessons" has enabled me to regularly over-achieve sales plans, receive numerous promotions to leadership positions, and win numerous President's Clubs Awards trips, MVPs, and Sales Rep of the Year awards.

Knowledge is power.

And the application of knowledge is wisdom.

Knowing what the most Elite Sales Pros do on a regular basis is vital if you desire to become an Elite Sales Pro!

I hope that this little book helps to better inform, encourage, and inspire you to greater heights in your sales career and in every other area of your life where you are engaged in the fine art of relationship building and persuasion!

So read it and DO it!

Gregg

1

Use The Front Door

Treat your customers as you would any neighbor. You would never use a neighbor's garage door or back door. So why would you not use your customer's "front door." Too many sales people avoid the gate keeper and sneak their way in and out of accounts. Successful Sales Pros go right to the front door…all the time. They properly identify themselves when entering an account and usually have a set appointment and leave the account by saying a proper goodbye. Do you use the front door?

2

Humility is Key

No matter how good you think you or your product/service are, remember that a humble demeanor is and will always be the most attractive quality any Sales Pro can possess. Remember that even though your product/service is the most important thing to you, it may not be the most important thing to your customer. Keep that in mind when conversing with customers. It will build a huge trust factor. Do you think your customers would describe you as humble?

3

Bring Value to Every Customer

Bringing in donuts and coffee are always appreciated. But you are cheating your company and customer if you are not consistently providing value on every sales call you make. Whether it's product information, or competitive updates, your goal should be to deliver something of value to as many of your customers as possible as frequently as possible. Are you adding value on every sales call you make?

4

Appropriate Follow Up is Key

Successful Sales Pros are constantly following up with their customers either by phone, text, or e-mail. Consistent follow up--even just simple hand written "thank you" notes--puts closure on each sales call and sets the proper expectations for "next steps" for you and the customer. Sales Pros also follow up as soon as possible on every action item. If they receive a customer request, they attempt to answer the request immediately. Are you following up with every one of your customers after each sales call?

5

Failure to Prepare is Preparation for Failure

Most sales people wing it. They have a vague goal in mind of what they want to achieve, but frequently fail to thoroughly prepare for customer meetings. Successful Sales Pros thoughtfully tailor their presentation to the specific personality, needs and concerns of the customer. They anticipate likely objections and have well thought out succinct answers for them. Are you adequately preparing daily for every sales call or do you wing it? Do you have a quarterly or annual business plan in place that you are constantly tracking and evaluating?

6

If You Can't Say It In 4 Words of Fewer, Don't Say It

I know I just used 13 words to say that. But concise communication whether oral or written in this day and age is vital to the success of any aspiring Sales Pro. Successful Sales Pros are always thinking about the easiest and most concise way to communicate a thought. The fewer words you use, the less the chances for any potential miscommunication which could potential side-track or derail a deal. Brief communication demonstrates respect for the customer's valuable and limited time. Are you respectful of your customer's time? Do you review all e-mails, voice mails, and texts prior to sending?

7

Cultivate Partnerships Not Customers

The most successful Sales Pros are always looking for ways to build relationships based on integrity and trust. A customer is somebody who buys from you once. A partner is a customer who thinks of you as more than just someone providing a good or service. A partner is a customer who believes you have a vested interest in his or her business success and who is committed to yours. Do you have customers or partners?

8

Successful Leaders Serve Others

Successful Sales Pros are not selfish. They are *selfless*. Constantly putting other people's needs ahead of their own. Successful Sales Pros are always looking for ways to help their customers and teammates achieve their goals. They are looking to make others successful knowing their own success will follow. Are you a servant leader who is maniacally focused on the needs of others?

9

Show Gratitude

Sales Pros possess a spirit of gratitude and are constantly thanking their co-workers and partners. Sales Pros appreciate their successes and are even grateful for the lessons learned from their failures. They tend to see a glimmer of hope in every situation and tend to radiate that gratitude to everybody around them. People like to buy from people who greatly appreciate their business. Think of how great it feels when people tell you how much they appreciate you. How often do you tell your customers how much you appreciate them?

10

After You Close The Deal, Shut Up

The most successful Sales Pros know when they close the deal it's time to shut up and change the topic of conversation before they say something that may cause the customer to change his mind. After you have gained the customer's commitment, it's best to change the subject as soon as possible. Do you know how to shut up after you close the deal?

11

People Buy From People They Like

If two products or services are similar, customers will almost always make their selection based on what sales rep they like more. We go out of our way to spend time with those we like most. It's no different in the sales world.
Do your customers like you?

12

Focus on Your Customer's Pain Points

If you have not adequately addressed this for your customer, chances are you will probably not get the sale. The most successful Sales Pros are able to determine what is most important to their customers and tailor their presentations accordingly. Every customer has a unique need. Most reps fail to adequately pinpoint the unique needs of their customers and how your product or service can best serve them. The best Sales Pros ask the right questions to identify unique needs and "pain points" to most effectively customize their sales presentations accordingly to best meet those needs and alleviate those "pain points." Are you doing this?

13

Less Telling More Selling

The most successful Sales Pros spend the majority of their time with customers asking High Value Questions to determine exactly what the customer's main needs and concerns are. "Telling" your customers what your product/service can do is important. But before you can do that, you must first determine the major needs and concerns of the customer. What primarily drives them? The best way to ascertain this information is to ask. The most highly effective Sales Pros listen twice as much as they talk. How effective are you at asking High Value Questions with your customers and then actively listening to their responses?

14

Sales is a Process Not An Event

The sales process is dynamic and organic and consists of an approach, a body (features and benefits), proof and a close. While successful Sales Pros are always listening closely for buying signs and always ready to close the sale, it's not always an appropriate time to be closing the sale. Many times, sales people will rush the close prior to adequately qualifying and overcoming the customer's needs and concerns. Rushing the close often times makes sales people come across as desperate and can scare the customer away. The best Sales Pros go through the entire process in a disciplined thoughtful manner and never rush the close. Do you rush the close and have deals fall through as a result or do you go through the complete sales process?

15

Always Have Lots of Irons in the Fire

Successful Sales Pros always have a lot in their sales "pipeline." Proactively cultivating a large "prospect list" enables successful Sales Pros to constantly have a list of new business prospects they can develop when current business is closed and more established business dries up or falls through. Even if some of the pipeline leads are not as developed, the Elite Sales Pros are always working on advancing them to the next level of the sales process. How big is your pipeline? Do you have one?

16

Never Criticize Your Competition

While it is vital to distinguish your product or service from the competition, never refer to your competition in a defamatory way. Focus on your product's positive features and benefits and avoid speaking negatively about the competition even if your customers do. While it may be tempting to criticize your competition, discipline and humility ultimately get rewarded. Do you ever slam your competition?

17

Know the Decision Maker

All successful Sales Pros possess the ability to determine who the key decision makers are so they don't "spin their wheels" spending too much time with customers with limited/no influence on the ultimate purchasing decision. Often times, there will be multiple people/decision makers. Determine who they are and find out what their specific needs/potential objections are to maximize the opportunity of closing the sale. Are you focused on the key decision makers or spending too much time with people with little or no influence on actual purchasing decisions?

18

You Don't Need to Kick the Door Down. Just Get a Foot In It

The top Sales Pros never accept no for an answer. They know that the best way to get into the most difficult accounts is by getting a foot in the door. They know instinctively that once they get access to the account they can build on "small wins" and build the business incrementally. Those who bully their way into an account like a bull in a china shop, almost always fail. Don't be that guy or gal! How do you approach your customers?

19

Attitude Determines Altitude

I've never met a truly successful Sales Pro who doesn't exude positive energy and enthusiasm. They tend to frequently have a smile on their faces in spite of the circumstances. They are the "calm in the storm" type of people. The sales process can be full of failures and rejection. Nevertheless, true Sales Pros persevere and stay positive in the midst of it all. They view the rejection as temporary and are always looking for ways to find alternative approaches to achieving success. If you understand that failure and rejection are the norm, you can accept it and stay positive, knowing that in the end, you will prevail! When you chose to smile in the midst of the storm you'd be surprised how that positive attitude you've chosen to possess and convey can positively transform the environment around you. How is your attitude?

20

Half-Heartedness Always Results in Defeat

Customers can sense true commitment, conviction and confidence. If you want your customers to be confident in your product, it has to start with you. If you have doubts about your own products/services, chances are your customers will too. There is no middle road. True Sales Pros exude a confidence that is contagious. Decide for yourself that what you are selling is the best solution for the customer and let that enthusiasm and conviction be reflected in all your customer exchanges and interactions. If you do, your customers will be far more likely to feel it themselves. Do you exude confidence and enthusiasm in all your customer interactions?

21

Always Acknowledge and be Respectful of Customer's Time

One of the things that bothers customers the most is when sales reps don't acknowledge their customer's time. If the customer is not engaged because they have other things on their mind, they are far less likely to receive and internalize the information you are sharing (no matter how significant it may be). One highly effective technique you can incorporate with your customers is to ask them directly, "Do you have a few minutes now to talk or is there a more convenient time later we can discuss x,y,z?" By prefacing your conversation with this simple question you are demonstrating to your customer that you understand their time is valuable which should help maximize customer engagement. When you talk with a customer, do you begin each conversation by asking them, "Do you have a few minutes to speak about x,y,z issue?"

22

Never Be at a Loss for Words

Always plan what you are going to say with your customers. Successful Sales Pros are always anticipating questions they may be asked and preparing a succinct answer or statement to help move the sales process along. For example, if you know that one of your customers is finishing some work and will have a few minutes to speak with you prior to another meeting, plan out what you will say to them as succinctly as possible which should include the 2 or 3 most important things you want to convey. That way you communicate the most vital information in as short a period of time as possible and always leave opportunities for expanded discussions at the customer's discretion. Do you plan and rehearse your conversations prior to meeting with your customers?

23

Always Be Prepared to Discuss, "What's New" With Your Customers

I can't tell you how many times I've seen sales people who have been asked, "What's new" by their customers respond by saying, "oh, nothing much. Everything is pretty much the same" or something similar that misses the opportunity. The most successful Sales Pros always have a succinct and powerful answer which frequently piques customer interest and leads to more customer engagement and expanded discussion. You should never be at a loss when asked, "What's new?" Are you?

24

Eye Contact is Vital

Eye contact engenders personal trust and confidence. Looking down and not establishing direct eye contact can imply distrust. Successful Sales Pros cultivate trust with their customers and do their best to always establish eye contact in one-on-one conversations and with groups. It sounds simple, but you would be surprised how many people in sales don't establish direct eye contact with their customers. Do you make good eye contact?

25

People Love to Hear Their Own Name

Don't ever under-estimate the significance of using people's names as frequently as possible. It gets people's attention and lets them know you know their name and implies that you are tailoring your presentation personally to them. If you want to cultivate relationships with your customers built on trust, use their names whenever possible. Do you know all your customers' names? How often do you use them when interacting with your customers?

26

Superficial Discussions Usually Result in Superficial Understanding

Average sales reps speak in generalities. They frequently fail to ask the type of "high value questions" to their customers that lead to more in depth discussions and subsequently fail to identify real needs and concerns. Seasoned Sales Pros go deep in their conversations with their customers. Their goal is for their customers to possess a thorough understanding of their product or service and frequently use powerful examples, analogies and illustrations to reinforce their key product or service features and benefits. Do you keep it superficial?

27

Rejection is Normal in Sales

The way one handles rejection is as important, if not more important, than the way one handles success. It's easy to be full of joy and enthusiasm when things are going your way, but the true test of your integrity and character—the stuff that's inside you—is when you are faced with challenges and obstacles. Just remember that your customers are taking note of how you handle rejection and will have a considerably higher opinion of you if you handle it in stride. Sales Pros expect rejection to be a normal part of their day and use rejection as an opportunity to demonstrate patience, composure and maturity to their customers. How do you handle rejection?

28

Asking the Right Questions Provides an Opportunity to Inform and Educate

The most successful Sales Pros understand that the best way to convey information is to allow their customers to come to their own conclusion. Nobody likes to be told what to believe and what not to believe and be forced into buying something. The most satisfied and loyal customers are those who have a thorough understanding of the good or service they are using. Asking "high value questions" related to the good or service you are selling allows the customer to think through how the product/service works and how it can best meet their needs. It's always more powerful when the customer reaches his own conclusions about your product or service verse your telling them. Asking questions is a lot less potentially threatening than detailing your product/service to the customer. When customers are being asked questions, they are being engaged. An engaged customer is one who is selling themselves on your product or service. Are you asking thoughtful "high value questions" that allow you to inform them by engaging them?

29

Set 1-2 Minor Goals Daily and Accomplish Them Before Noon

I know that on its face this may seem somewhat basic and insignificant. But you would be surprised at how many sales professionals rarely if ever set minor daily goals. While the sales professional may have 10 major quarterly sales goals, rarely does the sales professionals set 1-2 minor goals per day to help them achieve these major 10 quarterly goals. Setting and accomplishing the 1-2 minimum minor daily goals is crucial in achievement of the 10 or so quarterly goals. If you can accomplish 2 minor goals that you MUST accomplish as early as possible each day, you will have accomplished 40 minor sales goals every month (based on 20 sales days/month) and 120 every quarter! The goals you set should be SMART Goals (Specific, Measurable, Attainable, Realistic, & Timely). Successful Sales Pros are focused on accomplishing as many minor goals as possible every day as they understand that accomplishment of these goals always translates into achievement of the MAJOR goals. Are you setting and achieving 1-2 minor sales goals per day?

30

Simplify the Sales Process

Elite Sales Pros know how to get to "yes" in the shortest amount of time possible. One of the main reasons is that Elite Sales Pros are very proficient at simplifying the sales process for their customers. The more steps that are involved in the sales process, the more complicated the process becomes and the more likely the process is likely to get delayed or derailed. Elite Sales Pros make it very easy for their customers to order their product or service even if the process requires multiple steps. Are you simplifying the sales process for your customers?

31

Person to Person Communication is Generally Always the Best

While a great deal of communication is done via e-mail and text some dealings are best accomplished in person, face to face. Elite Sales Pros know that there is no substitute for face to face conversations. A lot can be lost in translation via e-mail and text especially if you don't know the customer with whom you are communicating that well. Personal meetings may require more time to schedule but frequently result in significantly more being accomplished than e-mail/text/phone communications. One of the primary reasons for this is that personal interactions allow for the Sales Pro to read the customer's body language and "break the ice" by generating light conversation around some of the customer's main areas of interest outside of work. Customers also tend to appreciate the personal interaction and time the Sales Pro took to schedule and dedicate to the meeting. It lets your customer know they are important enough for you to carve out part of your day to meet with them. How much time do you dedicate to meeting with your customers in person?

32

Optimize "Down Time"

I can't tell you how frequently I walk into accounts and see the sales person distracted with social media or games. Successful Sales Pros are always advancing either the sales process, a relationship, or their own professional knowledge and skill sets. Successful Sales Pros are seldom bored. They know how to optimally manage their time and try to cram as much as they can into each day. If there is "down time" in between sales calls, Sales Pros are busy on e-mail, text, and the phone following up on past sales calls, confirming and setting up future appointments. They are always moving the ball forward and tend to frequently say, "there's never enough time in the day." What type of activities are you doing during your "down time" during the day?

33

Minimize Power Point Whenever Possible

Studies have demonstrated that people don't retain large amounts of information communicated via power point slides/presentations. Some refer to these types of large Power Point slide deck presentations as "death by Power Point." Of course, there is sometimes a need to show an important slide or visual image which can be very effective. But in general, try to keep your power point presentations to a minimum. While visuals may at times enhance the presentation especially when communicating the features and benefits of technically sophisticated products, procedures or systems, there is no substitute for personal eye-contact and interaction with your customers. You need to be the main attraction in any sales presentation, not your power point slides. Are you?

34

Focus on Common Interests and Experiences with Your Customers

An old sales manager once told me that no one cares how much you know until they know how much you care. Elite Sales Pros are masters at cultivating deep relationships with their customers. Not superficial ones. And they do this by taking an active interest in their customer's lives by finding out what their customers are interested in and using those common interests to forge a genuine friendship and trust. Sales is really about relationships and the most Elite Sales Pros are the best at making friends. They understand that this requires more time and effort but understand that the long term payoff is enormous. Most of my best relationships were developed and galvanized with my customers outside of work where I could really get to know them on a much deeper level. How much time every month do you spend cultivating relationships with your customers outside of work?

35

Be Open and Ask for Constructive Criticism from your Customers and Colleagues

One of the hardest things in life is to acknowledge our own shortcomings, and weaknesses. Sadly, however, most sales professionals never become Sales Pros because they rarely if ever worked on their greatest flaws. The most personal and professional growth I've ever experienced came as the result of asking my most trusted colleagues and customers for an honest assessment of not only my greatest strengths but also my greatest weaknesses. I wouldn't recommend asking all your customers what your greatest flaws are but I would recommend asking one or two whom you really respect and who you know will provide an honest assessment. You may have a glaring deficiency that everybody else in the world can see besides you. And that deficiency either in your character, behavior or ability may be what inhibits you from becoming the Elite Sales Pro you've always wanted to be. Elite Sales Pros engage in intense personal assessments and acknowledge and improve on their weaknesses. They are constantly growing and developing. Are you?

36

Have Difficult Conversations With Your Customers

This one took me years to figure out. But one of the best things you can ever do to become the Elite Sales Pro you desire to be is to get comfortable being uncomfortable. Elite Sales Pros know that closing the sale frequently requires achieving a consensus among a group of customers and influencers. They know that it is very rare for everyone involved in the sales process to be "on board." They know that there are always a few influencers that are more difficult to deal with who can potentially disrupt or even halt the sale. Most sales professionals avoid these people at all costs and try to go around them. But the Elite Sales Pro knows instinctively that in order to close the sale, that he will have to interact personally with the most difficult customer(s). He knows if he can get that person(s) on board that there is a high likelihood that he will close the sale. It takes courage to have difficult conversations with your most intransigent customers. But I can assure you that if you make a concerted effort to do so, you will gain confidence and reap the rewards. Do you avoid your most difficult customers or do you engage them directly?

37

Be Nice Even When You Don't Feel Like It

Sales can be a grind and it's easy to get discouraged for any number of reasons. But Elite Sales Pros "fake it till they make it." They recognize that no matter what challenges they are facing in the background, they can't allow their customers to sense their unhappiness or frustrations. I've found that no matter how down I may be feeling, when I choose to smile at others, the world tends to smile back at me. If you find yourself getting consumed with negative feelings, doubts and frustration, I would challenge you to put on a smile to the outside world and observe how your mood and circumstances tend to change. Customers don't want to be around much less buy from a miserable person. Make it a habit to treat everyone with whom you come in contact with warmth and kindness as much as possible and observe how your own mood (and your customers') brightens. How much warmth and kindness do you exude to your customers?

38

Find Out What the Most Successful Sales Reps With Whom You Work Are Doing

Elite Sales Pros are always seeking to improve themselves personally and professionally. They tend to be humble and open to learning new skills and approaches. They are constantly "working on their game"—constantly trying to gain an edge. One of the best ways to progress as a sales professional is to reach out to other top performers from your company or perhaps even Sales Pros from another company or industry to find out what their keys for success are. I have done this throughout my career and have been able to gain a great deal of key information, tips and techniques that I've applied to enable me to achieve success. Are you reaching out to the most successful people with whom you work?

39

Be Your Own Unique Self

This sounds simple and perhaps a tad cheesy, but I've found that many of the sales reps with whom I come in contact are trying to emulate other people and come across as insincere and too stiff. Elite Sales Pros are not afraid to be themselves no matter how quirky their personalities may be. They tend to be more down to earth and more transparent with their customers. As a result, they can develop stronger more meaningful relationships with their customers. Being yourself means being comfortable in your own skin with all your unique short-comings. If you are more introverted and analytical, don't try to be extroverted and vice versa. Be yourself. It will free you up and enable you to cultivate stronger relationships and trust with your customers. Are you acting like yourself with your customers or do you find yourself acting like someone else?

40

Don't Gossip and Associate With Negative Teammates

As noted previously, sales can be a grind and it can be easy to get down. And as the saying goes, "misery loves company." When you are not achieving your sales goals or are frustrated with your boss or sales plan, it can be easy to call another rep to commiserate. While it may be healthy to do so from time to time, recognize the fact that too many negative conversations with negative people can significantly impact not only your mood but also your performance. Elite Sales Pros minimize negative talk and gossip with teammates. They recognize that sales has its "ups and downs" and tend to surround themselves with positive people in their lives who will encourage them during challenging times. They also know that "bitch sessions" are counterproductive and that their time is better spent trying to figure out solutions. Would your peers generally describe you an encouraging optimist or discouraging pessimist?"

If you would like to have Gregg speak to your sales team or organization or order this book in bulk, please contact Gregg at **www.greggjackson.com**